CARING FOR LOGGERHEAD SEA TURTLE

Pet owners manual

A complete guide to their habitat, Care and ownership, dietary requirements, and lots more Guide

DR MORRIS HART

Table of Contents

Overview of Loggerhead Marine Turtles

Known by their scientific name, Caretta caretta, loggerhead sea turtles are amazing animals that live in the world's oceans. Being one of the largest species of sea turtles, they are important to marine ecosystems and are regarded as keystone species. In this extensive guide, we will explore the biology, behavior, habitat, conservation status, and issues related to owning loggerhead sea turtles as pets.

1. Biology and Taxonomy

Loggerhead sea turtles are members of the Cheloniidae family and are distinguished by their large heads and powerful jaws that allow them to consume a wide range of food sources, such as fish, crabs, mollusks, and jellyfish. Their shell is made up of bony plates that are covered in a layer of keratin known as scutes, which protects them from predators and environmental hazards.

2. Anatomy

With their large flippers that are designed for swimming, adult loggerhead sea turtles can easily navigate the ocean currents. Their carapace, or shell, is reddish-brown in color and has a distinctive heart-shaped pattern. They typically weigh between 80 and 200 kilograms (176 to 441 pounds) and measure between 90 and 110 centimeters (35 to 43 inches) in length.

3. Dispersion and Environment

With large nesting populations in the Atlantic, Indian, and Pacific Oceans, loggerhead sea turtles are found worldwide in subtropical and temperate waters. They migrate great distances between their foraging and nesting grounds, using ocean currents and magnetic fields to guide them. Their habitats include coastal regions, coral reefs, and offshore feeding grounds, where they are essential to the health of marine ecosystems.

4. Nesting and Procreation Practices

In order to lay their eggs, female loggerhead sea turtles return to their natal beaches, sometimes traveling thousands of kilometers across the ocean to reach their preferred nesting sites. Nesting usually takes place at night, with the females excavating large, sandy nests and depositing clutches of 100 to 150 eggs; once the nest is covered, the female goes back to the sea, leaving the eggs to hatch after about 60 days.

5. Dangers and the State of Conservation

The International Union for Conservation of Nature (IUCN) has classified loggerhead sea turtles as vulnerable due to the numerous threats they face in the wild, including habitat loss, pollution, climate change, bycatch in fishing gear, and poaching of eggs and adults for their meat and shells. Conservation efforts are being made to protect nesting beaches, lessen the impact of fishing, and increase public awareness of the importance of sea turtle conservation.

6. Reasons to Think About Keeping Pet Loggerhead Sea Turtles

A loggerhead sea turtle's long lifespan means that its owners must be committed to caring for it for the rest of their lives. Additionally, obtaining sea turtles from the wild can contribute to population declines, and keeping them as pets may be illegal in some jurisdictions. Despite the appeal of keeping a sea turtle as a pet, it is important to understand the complexities and responsibilities involved.

7. Final Thoughts

As a result of their unique needs and conservation status, loggerhead sea turtles are not recommended as pets for most people. However, there are numerous ways to support loggerhead sea turtle conservation efforts, ranging from advocating for the protection of marine habitats and nesting beaches to volunteering with sea turtle rehabilitation programs. Together, we can ensure a brighter future for these amazing creatures and the oceans they call home.

Chapter 1

A Legal and Ethical Perspective

In this section, we will examine the legal framework surrounding the ownership of loggerhead sea turtles and delve into the ethical dilemmas inherent in the exotic pet trade. Keeping a loggerhead sea turtle as a pet involves a number of legal and ethical considerations, from understanding the laws and regulations governing ownership to grappling with the ethical implications of keeping a wild animal in captivity. Prospective turtle keepers must carefully weigh their options.

1. Legal Structure

It is important for potential turtle keepers to become familiar with the laws and regulations that apply in their area before obtaining a loggerhead sea turtle as a pet.

The legal status of sea turtles varies greatly between jurisdictions. Some countries have strict laws in place to protect sea turtles and regulate their trade, while others may have lax enforcement or no regulations at all.

The Endangered Species Act in the United States and the Convention on International Trade in Endangered Species of Wild Fauna and Flora (CITES) worldwide are just two examples of national and international legislation that protects loggerhead sea turtles. These laws forbid the taking, trading, and use of loggerhead sea turtles and their byproducts, such as eggs, meat, and shells; breaking these laws can result in harsh punishments like fines, incarceration, and the confiscation of the turtle.

Moreover, sea turtles' conservation status as fragile or endangered species emphasizes the significance of ethical issues when considering their ownership as pets, even in areas where they are not specifically protected by law.

2. Moral Aspects

The moral conundrums raised by owning loggerhead sea turtles are related to conservation, sustainability, and animal care, among other things.

A home aquarium or enclosure may not be able to meet the complex physical, behavioral, and environmental needs of loggerhead sea turtles, which can lead to stress, boredom, and health issues due to inadequate living conditions, diet, and social interactions. a. Animal Welfare: Keeping a wild animal in captivity raises ethical concerns about its quality of life and welfare.

Conservation: Removing wild sea turtles from their natural habitats can disrupt breeding cycles, reduce genetic diversity, and weaken populations' resilience to environmental threats. While keeping a loggerhead sea turtle as a pet may seem harmless on an individual basis, the cumulative impact of the exotic pet trade can contribute to population declines and undermine conservation efforts. The global decline of sea turtle populations due to habitat loss, pollution, climate change, and human activities highlights the urgent need for conservation efforts.

Sustainability: In order to ensure the long-term survival of loggerhead sea turtles and other species, wild populations must be managed sustainably. The demand for sea turtles in the exotic pet trade can encourage illicit harvesting, poaching, and trafficking, further jeopardizing already vulnerable populations. Responsible ownership involves taking into account the ecological effects of keeping a loggerhead sea turtle as a pet and looking into alternative means of supporting conservation efforts that do not involve exploiting wild populations.

3. Non-Pet Ownership Options

Considering the ethical and legal challenges associated with keeping loggerhead sea turtles as pets, those who wish to promote sea turtle conservation can take into account the following options:

Volunteering is a great way for people to directly contribute to the protection of sea turtles and their habitats while also gaining valuable experience and knowledge. A lot of organizations and conservation groups offer volunteer opportunities to participate in sea turtle monitoring, research, and conservation projects.

b. Education and Advocacy: Educational outreach, community engagement, and advocacy campaigns can empower people to become stewards of marine ecosystems and champions for sea turtle conservation. Increasing public awareness of the significance of sea turtle conservation and the threats they face can help mobilize support for protective measures and policy initiatives.

c. Supporting Conservation Organizations: Another effective way to make a difference is to donate to well-known organizations and non-governmental organizations (NGOs) that are committed to the conservation of sea turtles. The money raised through these donations can be used to support habitat restoration, research projects, community outreach initiatives, and enforcement actions against poaching and illegal trade.

4. Final Thoughts

In summary, it is important for prospective turtle keepers to critically assess the implications of their choices and take into account the welfare of the animals involved as well as the broader ecological and ethical implications. By encouraging responsible stewardship, conservation awareness, and sustainable practices, we can work towards a future where loggerhead sea turtles and their habitats thrive in harmony with human activities. Keeping a sea turtle as a pet involves navigating a complex landscape of legal, ethical, and conservation considerations.

Chapter 2

Tank Requirements and Habitat Configuration for Loggerhead Sea Turtles

From the size and design of the tank to the water quality, temperature, and lighting, every aspect of the habitat plays a crucial role in ensuring the health and well-being of these magnificent creatures. In this comprehensive guide, we will explore the essential elements of habitat setup and tank requirements for loggerhead sea turtles, offering helpful advice and suggestions for creating a safe and enriching environment. Loggerhead sea turtles require specific habitats that are tailored to their natural behaviors, physiological needs, and environmental requirements.

1. Dimensions and Style of Tank

As large, active swimmers, loggerhead sea turtles require spacious enclosures to accommodate their size and allow for natural behaviors like swimming, diving, and exploring. A general rule of thumb is to provide at least 300 to 500 gallons of water per adult turtle, with larger tanks preferred whenever possible. The size and design of the tank are critical factors in providing adequate space and enrichment for loggerhead sea turtles.

Take into account the following aspects when constructing the tank:

Dimensions: To optimize swimming space and reduce stress, choose a rectangle or oval-shaped tank that is sufficiently long, wide, and deep to provide unhindered mobility and exploration.

Land Area: Construct a dry land area or basking platform using non-toxic materials like rocks, sand, or artificial platforms so the turtle may rest, bask, and control its body temperature.

Substrate: Steer clear of substrates that could be ingested or impaction-prone, including small rocks or sharp objects, and instead use fine sand, gravel, or broken coral, which simulate the sandy or rocky bottom of the ocean.

Hiding Spots: Utilize man-made or natural structures, like caves, rock formations, or PVC pipes, to create hiding spots within the tank where the turtle can seek refuge and feel safe.

2. Filtration and Water Quality

The health and well-being of loggerhead sea turtles depend on maintaining good water quality. Low water quality can cause respiratory infections, shell rot, and skin illnesses, among other health issues. To guarantee ideal water quality, take into account the following factors:

Filtration: For optimal efficacy, install a high-quality filtration system that can handle the tank's water volume and remove waste, debris, and hazardous pollutants. Select a filtration system that combines mechanical, biological, and chemical filtration components.

Water Parameters: Use dependable water testing kits to periodically evaluate water quality and make required adjustments. Monitor and maintain acceptable water parameters, such as temperature, pH, salinity, and ammonia levels, within the recommended range for loggerhead sea turtles.

Water Changes: Depending on the size of the tank and the number of turtles, replace between 25% and 50% of the water volume every two to four weeks in order to flush out collected waste and restore vital minerals and nutrients.

3. Light and Temperature

As ectothermic reptiles, loggerhead sea turtles depend on outside heat sources to regulate their body temperature and metabolism. Establish a thermally gradient environment within the tank to allow the turtle to move between warm and cool areas as needed. Proper temperature and lighting conditions are essential for the health, metabolism, and behavior of these marine animals.

Basking Temperature: To enable the turtle to thermoregulate and dry off after swimming, keep the basking area at 85 to 95°F (29 to 35°C). If extra heat is required, use infrared heat bulbs, ceramic heat emitters, or basking lamps.

Water Temperature: Use submersible aquarium heaters or in-line heaters to keep the water temperature consistent throughout the tank. Keep the water temperature between 75 and 85°F (24 and 29°C), with small changes to replicate real ocean conditions.

UVB Lighting: To encourage the production of vitamin D3 and calcium metabolism in loggerhead sea turtles, provide UVB lighting with a wavelength of 290 to 320 nanometers. Full-spectrum UVB fluorescent or mercury vapor bulbs should be placed above the basking area to guarantee sufficient exposure to UVB radiation.

Photoperiod: Use automatic timers to control the lighting schedule and maintain consistent day-night cycles. Photoperiod: To replicate natural daylight cycles, provide a photoperiod of 10 to 12 hours of light followed by 10 to 12 hours of darkness each day.

4. Improvement of the Environment

To reduce boredom and stress and to promote physical and mental well-being, it is imperative to enrich the turtle's surroundings with naturalistic features, stimulation, and activities. Some ways to consider for enrichment are as follows:

Aquatic Plants: Add real or fake aquatic plants to the tank to create visual barriers, hiding spots, and cover. Use non-toxic plants like water lettuce, java ferns, and anubias that are appropriate for the turtle's habitat and water quality.

Floating Objects: To add more locations for resting and basking, add floating items to the tank, such as logs, driftwood, or floating platforms. Just make sure the floating items are well attached to keep them from toppling over or tangle with the turtle.

Foraging Activities: Encourage the turtle to investigate its surroundings and participate in active hunting and feeding behaviors by dispersing food items throughout the tank or concealing them inside enrichment items like puzzle feeders, foraging balls, or PVC tubes.

Behavioral Enrichment: Introduce new textures, fragrances, and objects into the tank to give the turtles opportunities for exploration, exercise, and social interaction. Rotate enrichment items frequently to keep the turtles interested and avoid habituation.

5. Upkeep and Sanitation

Create a regular maintenance program to make sure that every part of the tank is routinely observed and maintained. Cleaning and maintenance are crucial to maintaining the turtle's habitat clean, sanitary, and free of dangerous infections and toxins.

Cleaning Schedule: Use aquarium-safe cleaning products and adhere to manufacturer dosage and application instructions to thoroughly clean and disinfect the tank, substrate, decorations, and filtration equipment to get rid of algae, debris, and organic waste.

Water Testing: To guarantee stability and ideal conditions for the turtle, test water quality parameters including pH, ammonia, nitrite, and nitrate levels on a regular basis using dependable water testing kits. You should also check the water's salinity and temperature every day.

Filter Maintenance: Change filter media, cartridges, and sponges as needed to prevent clogging and preserve water purity. Clean and maintain the filtration system in accordance with manufacturer directions to guarantee maximum performance and efficiency.

Waste Removal: Use a siphon or aquarium vacuum to suction the substrate and remove debris from the bottom of the tank. Remove uneaten food, excrement, and other organic waste from the tank as soon as possible to prevent fouling of the water and bacterial contamination.

6. Concluding remarks

In conclusion, the process of creating a suitable habitat for a loggerhead sea turtle in captivity involves meticulous planning, close attention to detail, and a commitment to meeting the environmental, behavioral, and physiological needs of the turtle. Turtle keepers can guarantee the health, happiness, and well-being of their aquatic companions by providing a spacious and enriching tank environment, maintaining high water quality and temperature, and implementing regular maintenance and cleaning practices.

Chapter 3

Guidelines for Loggerhead Sea Turtle Nutrition and Feeding

As omnivorous reptiles with complex dietary requirements, loggerhead sea turtles need a balanced and varied diet that mimics their natural feeding habits in the wild. In this comprehensive guide, we will explore the feeding behaviors, nutritional needs, and dietary considerations for loggerhead sea turtles, offering helpful guidelines and recommendations for meeting their nutritional requirements in captivity. Ensuring proper nutrition is essential for the health and well-being of loggerhead sea turtles in captivity.

1. Consumption Patterns

When it comes to feeding, loggerhead sea turtles display a wide range of behaviors that are contingent upon their life stage, habitat, and the availability of prey. They are opportunistic feeders that take in a wide range of prey, such as fish, crabs, mollusks, algae, jellyfish, sponges, and changes in the seasons.

Loggerhead sea turtles kept in captivity may exhibit comparable feeding habits to those of their wild counterparts, such as:

- grazing: Eating the seagrasses and algae that grow in their natural habitat.
- Foraging: Using their strong jaws and keen beaks to hunt and catch prey.
- Eating carrion and leftover food that they come across in their surroundings is known as scavenging.

- Browsing: Gathering samples of various plants and prey to satisfy their dietary requirements.
- Giving suitable food alternatives and encouraging normal feeding patterns in captivity require an understanding of these feeding behaviors.

2. Needs for Nutrition

While loggerhead sea turtles' precise nutritional needs may vary depending on factors like age, size, activity level, and reproductive status, meeting their nutritional needs in captivity involves providing a balanced diet that supplies essential nutrients, vitamins, and minerals needed for growth, development, and overall health.

- Provide high-quality protein foods, such as fish, shrimp, crab, and squid. Protein is necessary for growth, tissue repair, and muscle development.

- Carbohydrates: Incorporate foods high in carbohydrates, such as fruits, vegetables, and aquatic plants, into your diet. They provide energy and fiber for metabolic processes and digestive health.

- Lipids: Provide insulation, energy, and necessary fatty acids for hormone production and cellular function. Provide seafood, krill, and fatty fish to meet lipid requirements.

- Vitamins and Minerals: For strong bones, healthy immune systems, and general well-being, make sure you get plenty of vitamins A, B, C, D, and E as well as calcium, phosphorus, and magnesium. You can also add foods high in these nutrients to your diet, such fruits, leafy greens, and calcium supplements.

3. Nutritional Factors

To guarantee nutritional sufficiency and variety in the food, take into account the following factors when creating a diet for loggerhead sea turtles kept in captivity:

Diet unique to Species: Adjust food choices based on the nutritional requirements and feeding habits of loggerhead sea turtles, taking into account their age, size, health, and natural habitat.

Variety: To guarantee nutritional diversity and prevent dietary deficiencies, provide a diversified and balanced diet that includes a wide range of prey items, vegetables, fruits, and supplements.

Whole Prey Items: Offer live or frozen-thawed prey items, such as fish, shrimp, crabs, and squid, to drive hunting and feeding instincts. This will recreate the natural feeding experience and encourage natural foraging behaviors.

Commercial Diets: Add premium commercial turtle pellets to the diet or use diets made especially for sea turtles; look for reliable brands that offer a balanced diet and satisfy the dietary requirements of loggerhead sea turtles.

Gut loading is the process of enriching live prey with nutrient-dense meals like leafy greens, vegetables, and vitamin supplements prior to feeding the turtle. This process increases the nutritional content of the prey and guarantees that the turtle gets the vitamins and minerals that it needs.

Calcium Supplementation: To promote bone health, shell formation, and the prevention of metabolic bone disease, provide calcium supplements or meals high in calcium, such as cuttlebone, bone meal, or calcium blocks.

Feeding Frequency: Adult loggerhead sea turtles should be fed two to three times a week, with the frequency of feedings adjusted according to the turtles' specific nutritional needs, activity level, and metabolism. Juvenile turtles may need more frequent feedings in order to support their growth and development.

4. Feeding Methods

To guarantee adequate nutrition and avoid overfeeding or underfeeding, feeding loggerhead sea turtles in captivity necessitates meticulous planning, observation, and monitoring. Take into consideration the following feeding techniques and strategies:

Observation: Keep a close eye on the turtle's eating habits, appetite, and overall health to determine its nutritional status and make any necessary dietary adjustments. Watch for any odd behavior, lethargy, or weight loss that could point to a nutritional deficit or health issue.

Feeding Enrichment: Offer food items in a variety of shapes, sizes, and presentations to encourage natural feeding behaviors and to stimulate mental and physical activity. Use enrichment tools like feeding stations, puzzle feeders, and forage balls to encourage active feeding and exploration.

Hand Feeding: Carefully hand-feed a few food items to the turtle to establish a healthy feeding relationship and to offer treats as a reward for desired behaviors. Be cautious to prevent inadvertent injuries or bites from the turtle's sharp beak.

Scheduled Feedings: To help manage the turtle's metabolic and digestive processes, set up a regular feeding plan and routine that gives it stability and structure. Feed the turtle at the same time every day or on particular days of the week.

5. Concluding remarks

To sum up, providing loggerhead sea turtles with a healthy diet in captivity involves careful planning, close attention to detail, and a thorough understanding of their feeding habits and dietary requirements. Turtle keepers can guarantee the health, vitality, and longevity of their aquatic companions by providing a balanced and varied diet that consists of a combination of whole prey items, commercial diets, vegetables, fruits, and supplements. Proper feeding techniques, observation, and monitoring can help loggerhead sea turtles thrive in captivity and inspire admiration for their species and conservation in the wild.

Chapter 4

Veterinary Medicine and Health for Loggerhead Sea Turtles

To guarantee the health and welfare of loggerhead sea turtles kept in captivity, careful attention to detail, close monitoring, and access to veterinary knowledge are necessary. Proactive health care is crucial for ensuring the longevity and vibrancy of these magnificent marine reptiles. This includes everything from keeping an eye on environmental factors and water quality to identifying and treating medical problems. This thorough reference will cover all the essentials of loggerhead sea turtle health and veterinary care, including helpful advice and instructions for preserving health and handling frequent medical issues.

1. Keeping an eye on things and making observations

Health management for loggerhead sea turtles kept in captivity requires routine observation and monitoring. Caretakers can identify early indicators of disease or suffering and take immediate action by closely monitoring the individual's behavior, eating, and physical appearance. Create a regular monitoring schedule with the following items on it:

Every day, do visual assessments of the turtle's bodily condition, the integrity of its shell, its eyes, nostrils, and demeanor. Keep an eye out for any anomalies, such as lesions, wounds, swelling, discharge, or adjustments to your appetite or degree of activity.

Water Quality Monitoring: Use dependable water testing kits to periodically test and monitor water quality parameters like temperature, pH, salinity, ammonia, nitrite, and nitrate levels. Keep the water's quality at its ideal level to avoid stress, illness, and health issues.

Behavioral Monitoring: To gauge a turtle's general health and well-being, watch its swimming habits, eating habits, basking routines, and social activities. Keep an eye out for any indications of odd behavior, stress, hostility, or lethargy that could point to underlying health problems.

2. Veterinary Medical Attention

For the purpose of offering thorough veterinary care and medical attention when necessary, it is imperative to establish a relationship with a licensed reptile veterinarian with expertise in sea turtle medicine. Work with a veterinarian to create a personalized health care plan that addresses the unique requirements of the turtle. This plan should cover regular check-ups, diagnostic procedures, and available treatments. The following procedures could be part of loggerhead sea turtle veterinary care:

Physical Examinations: Arrange for a veterinarian to perform routine physical examinations on a turtle to evaluate its general health, physical state, and vital signs. Examine the skin, shell, eyes, mouth, and cloaca thoroughly to look for any anomalies or symptoms of disease.

Diagnostic Testing: To assess the turtle's internal health, identify underlying medical issues, and inform treatment decisions, conduct diagnostic tests such as bloodwork, fecal analysis, radiography, ultrasound, and microbiological cultures.

Treatment and medicine: In order to address particular health conditions including infections, injuries, parasites, metabolic disorders, or nutritional deficiencies, give your pet the proper treatment and medicine as directed by a veterinarian. Pay close attention to the directions provided by the veterinarian on treatment duration, dose, and administration.

Surgical Intervention: When conservative treatment is ineffective for severe medical issues such tumors, blockages, or shell fractures, surgical intervention may be necessary. To learn more about the advantages, disadvantages, and possible results of surgical operations, speak with a veterinarian who specializes in sea turtle surgery.

3. Typical Health Concerns

Even while loggerhead sea turtles are typically tough and durable creatures, both in captivity and in the wild, they can suffer from a variety of illnesses. Typical health problems in sea turtles kept in captivity could be:

Damage to the shell that results from trauma, collisions, or poor husbandry techniques includes abrasions, fractures, and abnormalities. In order to avoid infection, shell rot, or further issues, treat shell injuries very away.

Respiratory Infections: Coughing, wheezing, nasal discharge, or difficult breathing are symptoms of respiratory infections brought on by bacteria, fungus, or parasites. As instructed by a veterinarian, administer nebulization therapy, antibiotics, and supportive care.

Nutritional Deficiencies: Poor growth, weak shells, metabolic bone disease, or immunological dysfunction might result from nutritional deficiencies brought on by an inadequate diet, inappropriate feeding techniques, or metabolic problems. To correct nutritional imbalances, make necessary adjustments to the diet, supplements, and husbandry techniques.

The health and immune system of the turtle may be weakened by parasitic infestations, which include internal (nematodes, cestodes) and exterior (ticks, leeches, barnacles) parasites. Under veterinary supervision, give the recommended deworming or parasite treatments.

Trauma and Injuries: Serious injuries such as cuts, fractures, or amputations can be brought on by entanglement in fishing gear, boat strikes, predator assaults, or human activity. In order to encourage healing and minimize problems, provide supportive care, wound care, and pain control.

Environmental Stress: Factors like poor water quality, temperature swings, crowded living quarters, or unsuitable roommates can cause environmental stress, which can result in health issues like compromised immunity, increased vulnerability to illness, and aberrant behavior. To reduce stress and enhance wellbeing, take care of underlying stresses and improve the surroundings.

4. Preventive Medical Care

For loggerhead sea turtles to remain healthy, reduce the chance of disease, and increase longevity, preventive healthcare practices are crucial. Put the following preventative healthcare procedures into practice:

To stop the spread of contagious diseases and parasites, quarantine and adapt newcomers to their new surroundings before integrating them with the current population. While the turtles are in quarantine, keep a vigilant eye out for any indications of illness or stress.

Hygiene & Sanitation: Keep the habitat tidy and sanitary by routinely cleaning and disinfecting the filtration apparatus, decorations, substrate, and tank. Utilize cleaning supplies appropriate for aquariums and adhere to the dosage and application guidelines provided by the manufacturer.

Environmental Enrichment: To encourage mental and physical stimulation, lessen boredom, and stop stereotypical tendencies, provide enrichment activities, stimuli, and environmental enhancements. Provide chances to explore, swim, dive, and sunbathe in the tank habitat.

Nutrition and meal: Provide a varied and well-balanced meal that satisfies the nutritional requirements and dietary preferences of the turtle. Provide commercial diets, fruits, vegetables, whole prey items, and supplements to guarantee dietary diversity and avoidance of deficits.

Regular veterinary check-ups and health evaluations are recommended to monitor the turtle's general health, identify any early signs of illness or disease, and swiftly manage any medical concerns. Observe the advice given by the veterinarian regarding vaccinations, preventative care, and parasite management.

5. In summary

In conclusion, loggerhead sea turtles kept in captivity must have access to veterinary treatment and proactive health management in order to maintain their longevity and general health. Caretakers may support optimal health, identify and treat medical disorders, and give these amazing marine reptiles a high standard of care by putting preventative health care measures, routine observation, monitoring, and prompt veterinary intervention into practice. Loggerhead sea turtles can flourish in captivity and promote awareness of their species and conservation efforts in the wild with the right medical attention and management.

Chapter 5

Loggerhead sea turtles mental stimulation and enrichment

For loggerhead sea turtles kept in captivity to remain healthy and happy, enrichment and mental stimulation are essential. Because they are inquisitive and perceptive creatures, loggerhead turtles need chances for exercise, exploration, and mental stimulation in order to stay active, lower stress levels, and encourage their natural tendencies. This extensive tutorial will go over the value of enrichment for loggerhead sea turtles, cover a variety of enrichment methods and approaches, and offer helpful suggestions for raising the standard of living for captive turtles.

1. Comprehending Enrichment

The provision of stimulating settings, experiences, and activities that support the mental, emotional, and physical health of animals kept in captivity is referred to as enrichment. The goals of enrichment are to mimic natural behaviors, promote the development of problem-solving techniques, and offer chances for play, socialization, and exploration. Enrichment benefits loggerhead sea turtles in a number of significant ways.

Mental Stimulation: Prevents boredom and fosters mental health by stimulating the cognitive capacities, curiosity, and problem-solving abilities of the turtle.

Exercise: Promotes vigorous movement, exploration, and physical activity; it also helps to build muscle and improve cardiovascular and general fitness.

Behavioral enrichment improves the quality of life and contentment of turtles by encouraging their natural habits, which include swimming, diving, foraging, basking, and social engagement.

Environmental Variety: Encourages environmental exploration and adaptability by providing a wide variety of challenges, textures, odors, and stimuli within the habitat. This helps to avoid habituation.

2. Techniques of Enrichment

To improve the wellbeing of loggerhead sea turtles kept in captivity, caregivers can use a variety of enrichment methods and approaches. These methods fall into several categories of enrichment, such as:

Physical Enrichment: Offers chances for exercise, mobility, and environmental exploration. Options for providing loggerhead sea turtles with physical enrichment include:

- Build a roomy, dynamic tank environment with lots of space for swimming, diving, and exploring in your tank design. To replicate the turtle's natural habitat, include naturalistic elements like plants, caves, and tunnels.

- Install floating docks or basking platforms to create areas where turtles can relax, bask, and control their body temperature. To suit individual preferences, provide several places to bask in the tank at varying heights and locations.

Water Flow: To replicate the natural ocean currents and offer resistance for swimming and exercise, install water pumps, wave makers, or underwater currents.

Provide a range of substrates, including sand, gravel, rocks, and shells, so the turtle can explore and engage with a variety of textures and surfaces.

Sensory Enrichment: Offers sensory stimulation and a variety of environments by stimulating the turtle's senses of sight, smell, touch, and hearing. Options for providing loggerhead sea turtles with sensory enrichment include:

- Visual Stimuli: To draw the turtle's attention and promote exploration, place visual stimuli like mirrors, floating objects, or vibrant decorations.

- Scent Enrichment: To enhance the turtle's sense of smell and promote foraging habits, incorporate naturally occurring scents and odors into the habitat, such as seaweed, fish, or shrimp.

- Auditory Enrichment: To provide the turtle with a soothing and immersive auditory environment, play recordings of the ocean, waves, or marine life.

- Cognitive Enrichment: Using interactive tasks and puzzles, this program tests the turtle's capacity for problem-solving, memory, and cognitive skills. For loggerhead sea turtles, cognitive enrichment options could be as follows:

Foraging Toys: Conceal food items within floating balls, puzzle feeders, or enrichment equipment to entice turtles to hunt for, handle, and retrieve food through exploration and problem-solving.

Training Sessions: Use positive reinforcement training methods to teach the turtle basic actions and commands. To engage the turtle's cognitive abilities and reinforce desired behaviors, use treats, praise, and rewards.

Novel things: To encourage exploration and arouse the turtle's curiosity, add toys, manipulable things, or novel objects to the habitat. Provide a variety of objects with varying dimensions, weights, materials, and textures to provide both tactile and visual stimulation.

Social Enrichment: Facilitates social interactions and companionship between turtles, fostering natural behaviors and social bonding. Social enrichment strategies for loggerhead sea turtles may include:

- Tankmates: Introduce compatible tankmates such as other sea turtles, fish, or invertebrates to provide possibilities for social interaction, exploration, and group dynamics.
- Mirror Reflections: Place mirrors or mirrored surfaces outside the tank to provide the sense of social companionship and enhance the turtle's social behaviors and territorial instincts.
- Group Feeding: Feed numerous turtles together in a communal feeding session to foster social

interaction, competition, and natural feeding patterns.

3. Implementing Enrichment Practices

When implementing enrichment methods for loggerhead sea turtles, consider the following criteria and recommendations to guarantee safety, effectiveness, and positive outcomes:

Individualized Enrichment: Tailor enrichment activities and stimuli to the particular needs, interests, and talents of each turtle. Observe the turtle's response to varied enrichment options and modify accordingly to enhance engagement and happiness.

Rotation and Variation: To avoid habituation and preserve novelty and interest, rotate enrichment materials, activities, and stimuli on a regular basis. To maintain a fascinating and interesting environment for the turtles, occasionally introduce new enrichment alternatives.

Observation and Assessment: Pay careful attention to the turtle's activities, responses, and interactions with enrichment stimuli in order to evaluate the program's efficacy, enjoyment, and safety. Enrichment items that trigger hostility, tension, or negative reactions should be changed or removed.

Safety precautions: Make sure that all toys, buildings, and enrichment items are secure, non-toxic, and devoid of any small bits, sharp edges, or other potential hazards that could harm the turtle. To avoid mishaps or injuries, keep an eye on how people engage with enrichment materials.

Positive Reinforcement: To motivate the turtle to interact with enrichment activities and stimuli, use strategies such as snacks, praise, or prizes.

4. summary

In conclusion, loggerhead sea turtles in captivity need enrichment and mental stimulation to maintain their health, wellbeing, and natural behaviors. Caretakers can create an environment that is interesting and engaging for turtles, improving their quality of life and contentment, by providing a variety of enrichment alternatives including as physical, sensory, cognitive, and social enrichment. By implementing enrichment measures and using caution in their care, loggerhead sea turtles can flourish in captivity and serve as an inspiration for the preservation of their species in the wild.

Chapter 6

Possible Difficulties and Fixes for Petting Loggerhead Sea Turtles

Although having a loggerhead sea turtle as a pet can be gratifying, there are several issues and things to think about for those who take care of them. To maintain the health, wellbeing, and welfare of these amazing marine reptiles, caregivers must be equipped to handle a variety of problems, from addressing the turtle's complex environmental, nutritional, and social demands to negotiating legal and ethical issues. This thorough guide will examine some of the possible difficulties that come with owning loggerhead sea turtles as pets and offer helpful advice and workable solutions to help you get through these difficulties.

1. Compliance with Laws and Regulations

Narrowing the legal and regulatory path that leads to ownership of loggerhead sea turtles is one of the main obstacles to keeping them as pets. The Endangered Species Act in the United States and the Convention on International Trade in Endangered Species of Wild Fauna and Flora (CITES) worldwide are only two examples of national and international laws that provide protection for loggerhead sea turtles. Serious consequences, including as fines, incarceration, and the seizure of the animal, may follow violations of these regulations. To guarantee adherence to legal mandates:

Investigate Applicable Laws: Become acquainted with the rules, licenses, and permissions that control the possession, importation, and sale of loggerhead sea turtles in your region. Legal professionals, conservation organizations, or local wildlife authorities can provide advice on legal requirements and compliance procedures.

Get the Permits Required: Before obtaining a loggerhead sea turtle as a pet, make sure you have the necessary permits or licenses from the appropriate government agencies or wildlife authorities. Make sure you comprehend all of the permit's terms and conditions, particularly those pertaining to the turtle's ownership, transportation, and display limitations.

Ethical Considerations: Think about the possible effects on conservation efforts as well as the moral ramifications of retaining a wild animal in captivity. Consider whether keeping a loggerhead sea turtle as a pet is in line with the moral precepts of sustainable practices, conservation awareness, and responsible stewardship.

2. Needs for Housing and Habitat

Given their size, aquatic habits, and unique environmental requirements, loggerhead sea turtles in captivity can be difficult to house and properly care for. It takes careful planning to create the right habitat, taking into account elements like substrate type, lighting, temperature, water quality, tank size, and enrichment possibilities. In order to effectively solve housing and habitat challenges:

Size of Tank: Get an aquarium or tank that is roomy enough for swimming, diving, and sunbathing. Choose a tank big enough to fit the adult loggerhead sea turtle's size and activity level, taking into account that they can grow to be over three feet long and weigh over 300 pounds.

Water quality: Retain ideal levels of salinity, pH, temperature, ammonia, nitrite, and nitrate in the range that is suggested for loggerhead sea turtles. To guarantee clean, healthy water conditions, use high-quality filtration systems, frequent water testing, and standard maintenance procedures.

Environmental Enrichment: To encourage both physical and mental stimulation, add naturalistic elements, sensory experiences, and enrichment activities to the tank habitat. To create a dynamic and exciting habitat for the turtle, include interactive toys, caves, rocks, aquatic plants, and floating things.

Basking Area: Give the turtle access to a dry ground area or platform so it can relax, warm up, and control its body temperature. Make sure the turtle can comfortably rest in the accessible, stable, and spacious basking place.

Substrate and Décor: To replicate the natural ocean floor and provide the turtle a cozy and realistic habitat, use a substrate like sand, gravel, or crushed coral. To improve the tank environment and create visible obstacles, add decorations, hiding places, and shelter structures.

3. Nutritional Needs and Difficulties in Feeding

Due to their varied diet, unique nutritional requirements, and possible dietary preferences, loggerhead sea turtles can be difficult to feed when in captivity. For the sake of their health and wellbeing, it is imperative to provide a varied and well-balanced diet that closely resembles what they would naturally eat in the wild. To address dietary needs and difficulties with feeding:

Balanced Diet: To guarantee that the turtle has a balanced and nutritionally complete diet, provide it with a variety of prey items, vegetables, fruits, and vitamins. To create a meal plan that is specific to the needs, age, size, and health of your turtle, speak with a veterinarian or reptile nutritionist.

Whole Prey Items: To simulate a natural feeding environment and encourage natural foraging habits, include whole prey items in the diet of your turtle, such as fish, shrimp, crab, and squid. Provide fresh or defrosted game to pique the hunter's and feeder's instincts.

Commercial Diets: You can add premium commercial turtle pellets or diets made especially for sea turtles to your turtle's meal to supplement it. Select reliable products that satisfy the nutritional requirements of loggerhead sea turtles and offer balanced nourishment.

Nutritional Supplements: To address specific nutritional deficits or imbalances, provide calcium, vitamin, and mineral supplements as needed. Make sure that the suggested dosage and frequency guidelines are followed when administering supplements.

Feeding Methods: To encourage the turtle to eat and keep a healthy appetite, use a variety of feeding schedules, procedures, and presentation strategies. To determine nutritional intake and make necessary dietary adjustments, keep an eye on feeding habits, portion sizes, and food preferences.

4. Veterinary Treatment and Health Administration

Proactive medical treatment, regular health monitoring, and access to veterinary knowledge are necessary to ensure the health and well-being of loggerhead sea turtles kept in captivity. It is imperative to swiftly address health difficulties and medical issues in order to prevent disease, manage injuries, and promote general wellness. In order to successfully handle veterinarian care and health issues:

Build a Relationship with a Reptile Veterinarian: Locate and get in touch with a licensed veterinarian who specializes in sea turtle care. Plan for routine physical exams, health assessments, and veterinarian check-ups to keep an eye on the turtle's general condition and spot any indications of disease or other medical problems.

Diagnostic Testing: To assess the turtle's internal health, identify underlying medical issues, and inform treatment decisions, conduct diagnostic tests such as bloodwork, fecal analysis, radiography, and microbiological cultures. To create a diagnosis and treatment plan that is customized to the needs of the turtle, consult a veterinarian.

Treatment and medicine: In order to address particular health conditions including infections, injuries, parasites, metabolic disorders, or nutritional deficiencies, give your pet the proper treatment and medicine as directed by a veterinarian. Pay close attention to the directions provided by the veterinarian on treatment duration, dose, and administration.

Preventive Health Care: To reduce the risk of sickness, maintain optimal health, and encourage lifespan in captive turtles, implement preventive health care procedures such vaccinations, sanitation, quarantine, and parasite management. Develop a preventive health care plan with a veterinarian that is specific to the needs and conditions of your turtle.

5. Behavioral Difficulties and Environmental Enrichment

In a captive habitat, where space, resources, and artificial conditions may limit the turtle's options for exploration and stimulation, it might be difficult to provide environmental enrichment and encourage natural behaviors. Nonetheless, putting enrichment tactics and strategies into practice can assist in addressing behavioral issues and encourage a happy and comfortable environment for the turtle. In order to improve environmental enrichment and deal with behavioral issues:

Enrichment Activities: Provide a range of experiences, stimuli, and activities that appeal to the turtle's senses, support its innate habits, and stimulate its body and mind. To establish a dynamic and enriching environment, incorporate opportunities for physical, sensory, cognitive, and social enrichment into the turtle's daily routine.

Tank Design: Provide a home for the turtle that is as near to its natural habitat as possible, including elements like plants, rocks, caverns, hiding places, and different substrate alternatives that encourage exploration and interaction.

Social Interaction: Encourage friendship and social interaction by setting up group feeding times, introducing matching tankmates, and providing mirrors or reflected surfaces. Keep an eye on behavior and social dynamics to make sure everyone gets along and to avoid tension or violence.

Behavioral Observation: Pay close attention to the turtle's activities, responses, and interactions with enrichment stimuli in order to gauge its efficacy, enjoyment, and level of involvement. Based on the turtle's choices, interests, and behavioral responses, modify the activities and enrichment possibilities.

Environmental Variation: To avoid habituation and preserve novelty and interest, rotate and change enrichment items, activities, and stimuli on a regular basis. To maintain a fascinating and interesting environment for the turtles, occasionally introduce new enrichment alternatives.

6. In summary

In conclusion, raising loggerhead sea turtles as pets comes with a number of issues that need to be carefully thought out and requires caregivers to be very dedicated and well-prepared. Caretakers can guarantee the health, welfare, and well-being of these amazing marine reptiles in captivity by attending to legal and regulatory compliance, housing and habitat requirements, nutritional needs, veterinary care, and environmental enrichment. This will allow them to give a high standard of care. Loggerhead sea turtles can flourish as pets and species ambassadors with proper care, education, and conservation awareness, encouraging respect for their unique beauty, diversity, and significance in the marine ecosystem.

Chapter 7

Responsible Loggerhead Sea Turtle Ownership and Conservation Initiatives

Threats to the survival of loggerhead sea turtles include habitat loss, pollution, climate change, bycatch, and poaching. Therefore, conservation initiatives are crucial to safeguarding these famous marine reptiles for upcoming generations. In order to promote sustainable practices, raise awareness of the condition of loggerhead sea turtles, and support conservation efforts, responsible ownership of these marine animals in captivity is essential. We will examine the significance of loggerhead sea turtle conservation efforts, talk about appropriate ownership methods, and offer helpful advice for everyone who wants to assist sea turtle conservation in this extensive book.

1. Threats and the State of Conservation

The United States has designated loggerhead sea turtles (Caretta caretta) as a threatened species. According to the International Union for Conservation of Nature (IUCN), they are listed as vulnerable under the Endangered Species Act. Throughout their life cycle, these gorgeous marine reptiles are threatened by a variety of factors, such as:

Habitat Loss and Degradation: The availability of adequate nesting sites and foraging grounds for loggerhead sea turtles is threatened by human activities such as coastal development, habitat change, and destruction of nesting beaches.

Pollution: Through ingestion, entanglement, habitat destruction, and contaminated food sources, marine pollution—which includes plastic debris, oil spills, chemical pollutants, and marine debris—poses serious risks to loggerhead sea turtles.

Climate Change: Loggerhead sea turtle nesting sites, reproductive success, and food availability can all be impacted by rising sea levels, coastal erosion, ocean acidity, and changes in temperature and weather patterns.

Fisheries Bycatch: Worldwide, loggerhead sea turtles are seriously threatened by accidental capture in commercial fishing gear, such as trawls, longlines, and gillnets, which can result in injury, drowning, and even death.

Poaching and Illegal traffic: Despite legislative safeguards and conservation efforts, loggerhead sea turtle populations are nevertheless threatened in some areas by egg harvesting, adult turtle hunts for flesh and shells, and the illegal traffic in turtle products.

2. The Value of Conservation Measures

In order to protect loggerhead sea turtles and lessen the challenges they encounter in the wild, conservation initiatives are essential. The long-term survival and recovery of loggerhead sea turtle populations can be facilitated by stakeholders and conservationists working together on joint projects, enforcing protective measures, and tackling important conservation goals. Important conservation initiatives include the following:

Habitat Conservation and Restoration: By means of habitat conservation, restoration programs, and coastal management initiatives, important nesting beaches, foraging areas, and marine ecosystems are safeguarded and preserved.

Nesting Beach Monitoring: Monitoring nesting beaches systematically is necessary to keep tabs on nesting activity, evaluate population trends, and put conservation measures in place to shield nests, hatchlings, and nesting females from human interference, predation, and disruption.

Fisheries Management: Reducing the negative effects of commercial fishing operations on loggerhead sea turtles and other marine species by implementing rules, changing gear, and reducing bycatch.

Pollution Reduction: Reducing marine pollution and lessening the effects of plastic waste, oil spills, and chemical contaminants on loggerhead sea turtles and their ecosystems through the implementation of waste management plans, pollution control techniques, and public awareness programs.

Climate Change Adaptation: To lessen the effects of climate change on loggerhead sea turtle nesting locations, migration routes, and food supplies, strategies, habitat resilience plans, and ecosystem-based techniques must be developed.

Education and Outreach: Using educational programs, outreach campaigns, and community involvement activities, increasing public knowledge of the value of protecting sea turtles, encouraging responsible conduct, and cultivating stewardship.

3. Appropriate Ownership Techniques

Proper care of loggerhead sea turtles kept in captivity can be extremely beneficial to conservation efforts, bringing attention to concerns related to sea turtle conservation, and spurring action to save these amazing marine animals. In order to protect their welfare and advance environmental awareness, loggerhead sea turtles housed in captivity—whether in public aquariums, private collections, or educational facilities—need to be managed carefully and with ethical concerns. Several essential responsible ownership behaviors consist of:

Legal Compliance: Make sure that all local, state, federal, and international laws, rules, and licenses controlling the possession, importation, and commerce of loggerhead sea turtles are followed. Before obtaining a turtle as a pet, make sure you have all the licenses and permits required by wildlife authorities or conservation organizations.

Ethical Considerations: Assess the possible effects on conservation efforts as well as the moral ramifications of retaining a wild animal in captivity. When making judgments on the care and management of loggerhead sea turtles, take into account their natural habits, behavioral needs, and welfare needs.

Education and Outreach: To increase public understanding of sea turtle conservation issues, risks, and challenges, use captive sea turtles as ambassadors for their species. Provide interactive displays, explanatory signage, and educational events to engage visitors and raise awareness of conservation.

Contributions to Conservation: Provide funding, volunteerism, and advocacy to support research projects, conservation campaigns, and attempts to rehabilitate sea turtles. Make charitable contributions to respectable environmental groups, take part in citizen science initiatives, or lend a hand at nearby sea turtle rescue and rehabilitation facilities.

Husbandry and Care: To guarantee the health, welfare, and well-being of loggerhead sea turtles kept in captivity, provide them with excellent care, husbandry techniques, and habitat enrichment. To improve their physical and mental well-being, use best practices in housing, habitat management, feeding, veterinary treatment, and behavioral enrichment.

Public Involvement: Involve the community and the general public to promote respect, awareness, and reverence for loggerhead sea turtles and their environments. To inform guests about the biology, ecology, conservation, and threats facing sea turtles, plan guided tours, outreach programs, and public talks.

4. Useful Suggestions

Here are some useful suggestions for anyone who wants to encourage responsible ownership and sea turtle conservation:

Support Conservation Organizations: Contribute to respectable non-profit organizations, research centers, and conservation organizations that work to save the loggerhead sea turtle and its natural habitats. Think about endorsing programs that address pollution control, fisheries management, habitat preservation, and nesting beach conservation.

Opportunities for Volunteers: Offer your time, abilities, and knowledge to assist community-based programs, field research trips, and efforts aimed at protecting sea turtles. Take part in citizen science initiatives, volunteer activities, and beach clean-ups to support conservation efforts and benefit loggerhead sea turtle populations.

When visiting marine parks, conservation areas, and locations where sea turtles nest, it is important to engage in sustainable and ethical tourist practices. Respect local laws, ordinances, and conduct codes to reduce disruption, prevent habitat degradation for breeding birds, and observe proper wildlife viewing behavior.

To protect loggerhead sea turtles and their habitats, advocate for stricter environmental protection laws, regulations, and conservation efforts. Utilize social media campaigns, public awareness events, and educational outreach initiatives to increase public knowledge of sea turtle conservation issues, risks, and obstacles.

To safeguard loggerhead sea turtles and marine biodiversity, take personal actions to lessen your ecological footprint, minimize your Impact on marine ecosystems, and adopt ecologically friendly habits. To encourage ocean conservation, cut back on plastic usage, recycle waste, save energy and water, and choose sustainable seafood options.

5. In summary

To sum up, loggerhead sea turtle conservation initiatives and ethical sea turtle ownership are essential to safeguarding these amazing marine reptiles for coming generations. The long-term survival and recovery of loggerhead sea turtle populations around the world can be facilitated by individuals through the implementation of cooperative projects, the promotion of responsible behavior, the mitigation of critical conservation priorities, and support for habitat protection. We can cooperate to guarantee a better future for loggerhead sea turtles and to promote conservation knowledge and responsibility for our oceans and marine ecosystems through advocacy, education, and group action.

Chapter 8

In summary, the benefits of taking care of a loggerhead sea turtle

Taking care of a loggerhead sea turtle is an incredibly pleasant and rewarding activity that has several advantages for the turtle as well as the caregiver. The experience of taking care of a loggerhead sea turtle is full of memorable moments and chances for personal development, from developing a close bond with these magnificent marine reptiles to supporting conservation efforts and spreading awareness of their conservation requirements. We will examine the advantages of taking care of a loggerhead sea turtle in this final section, considering the good effects it can have on people, communities, and the larger preservation of marine biodiversity.

1. Individual Bonding and Connection

Making a close and lasting bond with these amazing creatures is one of the most fulfilling parts of being a caregiver for a loggerhead sea turtle. Caretakers and their turtles frequently develop a special link that is marked by affection, respect, and trust as they spend time together, observing, and tending to the turtle. This relationship builds a sense of camaraderie and companionship between the turtle and its caregiver that goes beyond species boundaries. Whether observing the turtle slither beautifully through the water, sunbathe indolently, or eagerly grab food from their fingers, caregivers are filled with happiness, amazement, and wonder that heightens their awareness of the intricacy and beauty of nature.

2. Awareness and Value of Education

Taking care of a loggerhead sea turtle offers an excellent opportunity to learn about the biology, ecology, behavior, and conservation of sea turtles. Caretakers acquire a deeper awareness of the distinctive adaptations, life history, and ecological value of loggerhead sea turtles through practical experience, observation, and research. Additionally, they grow more conscious of the dangers and difficulties that sea turtle populations face globally, such as habitat loss, pollution, climate change, and bycatch from fisheries. Caretakers may encourage action to preserve sea turtle habitats and guarantee their survival for future generations by sharing their knowledge and experiences with others. They can also inspire understanding and compassion for these amazing creatures.

3. Contribution to Conservation

Taking care of a loggerhead sea turtle enables caregivers to contribute significantly to efforts to save sea turtles and further the objectives of the conservation of marine biodiversity. Caretakers contribute to breeding programs, individual animal conservation, and research projects that deepen our knowledge of sea turtle biology and behavior by giving captive turtles a secure and caring environment. In order to help sea turtle rescue and rehabilitation facilities, nesting beach monitoring projects, and habitat conservation initiatives, caregivers can also take part in volunteer programs, fundraising campaigns, and conservation initiatives. Caretakers have the ability to positively influence loggerhead sea turtle populations and aid in their long-term survival and recuperation by working together.

4. Contentment and Welfare on an Emotional Level

In addition to providing emotional fulfillment and a sense of purpose and well-being, taking care of loggerhead sea turtles can also significantly improve the lives of those who provide care. A deeper connection to nature and a greater appreciation for the wonders of marine life are fostered by the daily interactions, obligations, and challenges connected with turtle care. These experiences bring one a sense of contentment and purpose. By lowering stress, worry, and sadness and offering chances for mindfulness, relaxation, and natural connection, taking care of a turtle can help improve mental and emotional health. Caretakers experience enormous joy and happiness as a result of witnessing the turtle grow and bloom under their care, which improves their overall quality of life and sense of fulfillment.

5. Motivation and Protest

Providing care for a loggerhead sea turtle has the potential to encourage caregivers to take up the cause of environmental stewardship and marine conservation, as well as to take action to save marine biodiversity and the seas. Caretakers can encourage others to get engaged, spread awareness of conservation challenges, and advance sustainable practices in their communities by sharing their stories and enthusiasm for sea turtle conservation. Through grassroots activism, public awareness programs, or social media advocacy, caregivers can have a significant impact on the future of our oceans and the creatures that live there by amplifying their voices. Caretakers may encourage good change and provide people the tools they need to take up the role of stewards of the marine environment by acting as advocates for the conservation of sea turtles.

6. Concluding remarks

To sum up, taking care of loggerhead sea turtles is a very fulfilling and enriching experience that has many advantages for both the turtles and the caregivers. The benefits of looking after a loggerhead sea turtle are numerous, ranging from creating chances for education and human relationships to supporting environmental advocacy and meaningfully contributing to conservation efforts. Caretakers can positively impact the lives of these amazing marine reptiles and support their protection and welfare by accepting the duties and challenges of turtle care with compassion, devotion, and commitment. When caregivers set out on the task of taking care of a loggerhead sea turtle, they join an international network of fervent people who are committed to safeguarding marine life for coming generations. We can guarantee a better future for loggerhead sea turtles and foster a greater understanding of the significance, diversity, and beauty of our oceans and marine ecosystems by working together and practicing shared stewardship.